GOOD TIMES, BAD TIMES

(and What the Neighbors Thought)

WRITTEN BY KATHLEEN KRULL

ILLUSTRATED BY KATHRYN HEWITT

HARCOURT, INC.

SAN DIEGO NEW YORK LONDON

I am indebted first to Sister Mary Jane, O.S. F., and then to the solid collection of music biographies at the Athenaeum Music and Arts Library of La Jolla; the Music Library, University of California, San Diego; and the San Diego Public Library.

Special thanks to Donna L. Keefe, L. Ac. —K. K.

www.HarcourtBooks.com

First Harcourt Paperbacks edition 2002

Library of Congress Cataloging-in-Publication Data
Krull, Kathleen.
Lives of the musicians: good times, bad times (and what the neighbors thought)/by Kathleen Krull;
illustrated by Kathryn Hewitt.
p. cm.
Summary: The lives of twenty composers and musicians, ranging from Vivaldi, Mozart, and Bach to Gershwin, Gilbert & Sullivan, and Woody Guthrie, are profiled in this eclectic, humorous, and informative collection.
Includes bibliographical references and index.
1. Musicians—Biography. I. Hewitt, Kathryn. II. Title.
ML385.K89 1993
780'.92'2—dc20 91-33497
[B]
ISBN 0-15-248010-2
ISBN 0-15-216436-7 (pb)

C E G I K J H F D B
I K J (pb)

Printed in Singapore

The illustrations in this book were done in Winsor & Newton watercolors on Winsor & Newton watercolor paper.
The display type was set in Goudy with Kuenstler Script initial caps.
The text type was set in Goudy.
Color separations by Bright Arts, Ltd., Singapore
Printed and bound by Tien Wah Press, Singapore
Production supervision by Sandra Grebenar and Wendi Taylor
Designed by Lisa Peters

To Ken, Carleton, and Kevin Krull

—K. K.

To Annelise, who sang before she could speak

—K. H.

Contents

Introduction

THE LIFE STORIES of famous musicians — Bach, Chopin, Tchaikovsky, Woody Guthrie — are familiar to many. But what were they like *really?*

What kind of children were they? How did they die? And what went on in between? What did they eat? What did they wear? How did they spend their money? What were their phobias, quirks, and bad habits? Who were their "significant others"? And what did the neighbors think? (Music is not a quiet career.)

Most interesting of all, what is it like to live a truly creative life? The musicians in this book, representing different countries, historical periods, and musical styles, do have things in common. About their music, they had a perseverance and single-mindedness that led not only to success, but also to eccentricities, sometimes amusing, sometimes sad.

Of all of them it could be said that their work shook up the times they lived in: It provoked riots (Stravinsky and Satie), led to death threats (Prokofiev), required police to control the crowds (Schumann), shaped entire generations of students (Boulanger), created wealthy superstars (Gilbert and Sullivan), was condemned as "addictive" and "immoral" (Joplin), and left blood on the piano keys (Gershwin). Music that we think of today as acceptable, "classic," or even staid often caused passion and controversy during its time. "Beethoven thought that through his music he could change the world," points out cellist Yo-Yo Ma. "Today, rock musicians are virtually the only ones who think that."

This music can still arouse emotion — and claim listeners. It's estimated that if Mozart were alive today, he'd be earning $20 million a year from sales of his records. The music, above all, is the reason people remember these musicians today.

Here, escorted by the patron saint of music, Saint Cecilia, are twenty lives, colorful and mysterious. These untold stories, never before collected in one volume, are offered now as a way of getting closer to the musicians — and the music.

—Kathleen Krull
San Diego, 1992

La Primava

The Red Priest

Antonio Vivaldi

born in Venice, Italy, 1678
died in Vienna, Austria, 1741

The most original and influential Italian composer of his generation, most famous for his 400 concertos, especially the Four Seasons

SUNNY, WARM VENICE WAS A PLACE where you couldn't get away from music. Gondoliers serenaded up and down the canals, fruit vendors whistled, shoemakers and shoppers sang from morning to night. Festivals, theaters, parties, and religious services required a constant supply of new music.

Antonio Vivaldi's father had big plans for him. He taught him the violin, got him a job as a violinist, and sent Vivaldi into the priesthood when the boy was fifteen years old. Father and son played duets at church. By the time Antonio was twenty-five and took a job teaching violin at the Pietà orphanage for girls, he was earning four times as much as his father.

Vivaldi was to spend most of his life at the Pietà.

Next to the big iron gate of the orphanage was a little nook in the wall, where every morning the porter checked for new arrivals. Orphaned or abandoned babies were given a home and taught music. The girls gave concerts that were a highlight of musical life in Venice. They sang "like angels" and played their instruments with great skill. It was said that the Pietà had the best-disciplined orchestra in

Italy at that time. Yet the girls were seldom seen. At concerts, they were hidden from the audience by an iron gate, possibly because some were deformed. Since they performed in a church, no applause was allowed, and people expressed enthusiasm by coughing, shuffling their feet, and blowing their noses loudly.

Vivaldi had to make sure everything ran smoothly. During intermissions, he would keep people entertained by playing his violin.

He had thick, curly red hair, and sometimes he wore red robes. More people knew him by his nickname—the Red Priest—than by his real name, but he did not seem especially "priestly." He didn't say Mass; he said that his weak condition—possibly asthma—prevented him from getting through a long religious service. But others said that he was forbidden to say Mass because he was always disappearing from the altar to jot down musical ideas.

Vivaldi may have been sickly, but he worked hard. He taught violin, conducted the orchestra, performed at concerts, and bought musical instruments for the school. Outside the orphanage, he toured in support of his own playing and composing. Vivaldi wrote music for all occasions; he was one of the most prolific composers in the history of music.

Vivaldi must have been full of energy and probably didn't have time to be temperamental. He didn't agonize over his work. He was deferential to those in authority and he never seemed to get in trouble.

Sometimes he was playful, putting little jokes in his music. He was terribly sensitive to criticism and was notoriously vain. He liked to boast about his fame, his rich patrons, and his ability to write music so quickly. Some people think he sometimes lied, saying he had written ninety-four operas, for example, when only forty-nine have ever been found.

Vivaldi was obsessed with money—he always asked the highest possible price for his music. But he also spent his money. When he died, at sixty-three, from a mysterious inflammation, he died poor, his music out of fashion.

Not until the music of Bach was rediscovered over a hundred years later and it was seen how much Bach respected the Red Priest did interest in Vivaldi's music revive.

♪ The *Four Seasons,* a set of four violin concertos, is one of the best-known works in Italian musical history. Parts of the music were meant to sound like turtledoves and goldfinches, flashes of lightning, a barking dog, fierce winds, and chattering teeth. (While for many people today this is Vivaldi's most beautiful work, it was also voted "Most Boring Composition" by New York radio listeners in 1984.)

♪ If Vivaldi was really in a hurry, he'd borrow tunes from his earlier music or from other composers. But then, so did other musicians of the time. One of Vivaldi's greatest admirers, Bach, borrowed some of Vivaldi's work and used it in his own compositions.

♪ In 1989, two of the top ten compact discs selling in England were of Vivaldi's music.

TWENTY CHILDREN AND 1,200 COMPOSITIONS

JOHANN SEBASTIAN BACH

BORN IN EISENACH, GERMANY, 1685
DIED IN LEIPZIG, GERMANY, 1750

German organist and great composer, best known for the Brandenburg Concertos, *the* Goldberg Variations, *and* The Well-Tempered Clavier

AS A YOUNG MUSIC TEACHER, Bach was out walking one night when six of his own students attacked him. They wanted an apology. Bach had called one of them a "nanny-goat bassoonist" — someone who makes a bassoon sound like a goat. But Bach wouldn't take it back; he drew a knife in self-defense. Luckily, the fight was broken up before anyone was really hurt.

All his life Bach had trouble with people who didn't see things his way. He once wanted to quit a job, and his employer, a duke, wanted him to stay. Bach was so insistent that the duke threw him in jail.

But here is the difference between Bach and the average stubborn person: during the month he spent in jail, Bach wrote forty-six pieces of music — music that we still listen to three hundred years later.

How could Johann Sebastian Bach have ever thought of becoming anything but a musician? His is the largest family tree in music. Almost all his male relatives were musicians — some seventy-six in all, fifty-three of them named Johann!

Bach's mother read him Bible stories, and his father taught him violin, sometimes late into the evening. But both parents were dead by the time Bach turned ten, and he went to live with a brother.

Bach was able to support himself before he was fifteen. He sang and took organ-playing jobs in towns near enough to walk to. (Bach was always a dedicated musician even if it meant blisters. Once he walked two hundred miles just to hear the great organist Dietrich Buxtehude play.)

Bach spent his whole life in one small part of Germany. He was married twice, first to his cousin, Maria Barbara, and after she died, to Anna Magdalena, who was a good singer and keyboard player. Anna Magdalena helped Bach in his work so much that her handwriting came to look just like his. Bach produced 1,200 musical works . . . and fathered twenty children (though only ten lived to adulthood). Five were named Johann, two Johanna, and four grew up to be famous composers themselves.

In his free time at night, Bach would sit in his armchair, smoking his pipe and drinking a beer, with a baby Bach on his lap as his wife and children played

and sang. Bach loved food and coffee (once he wrote a whole cantata about coffee). Among his most prized possessions were two silver coffeepots.

Bach was known as a dazzling organist. His strong legs pumped the pedals, his large hands performed acrobatics on the keyboard, and he'd even use a stick in his mouth to reach certain notes. But he wasn't a show-off. He said of his playing, "There is nothing remarkable about it. All you have to do is hit the right key at the right time and the instrument plays itself."

Later in life, Bach went blind, probably from copying out his own music in poor light for so many years. He died of a stroke at age sixty-five.

Hardly any of his music was published while he was alive, nor did he expect it to be. Bach did not think he was writing music for posterity. He was a professional—his music had an immediate purpose. Not until about a hundred years after his death did the genius of Bach begin to be widely recognized.

♪ Bach wrote the *Goldberg Variations* to relax a millionaire. One of his pupils, Johann Goldberg, worked for an insomniac count who needed music to get to sleep. The count sent the most generous payment Bach ever received.

♪ The famous *Two-Part Inventions* (or *Ideas*) were written for Bach's children, to exercise each finger and train the hands to play independently.

♪ The *Brandenburg Concertos* were a sort of job application to a court official of Brandenburg. Bach didn't get the job, but his concertos are today among the best-known instrumental works of this entire period.

♪ Mariane Ziegler, a poet who had published three books, supplied the words for several of Bach's works. In working with her Bach was ahead of his time, for women were allowed no public role in creating or performing music.

♪ The two *Voyager* spacecraft, launched into the solar system in 1977, contain three pieces by Bach, along with special record-playing equipment.

All°
19.

No Ordinary Baby

Wolfgang Amadeus Mozart

born in Salzburg, Austria, 1756
died in Vienna, Austria, 1791

Austrian composer who in his short life wrote many masterpieces, including symphonies, operas such as The Magic Flute *and* Don Giovanni, *and piano music*

UNTIL HE WAS THREE, Wolfgang Amadeus Mozart was an ordinary baby.

Then he began climbing up on the bench and imitating the clavier playing of his talented older sister Maria Anna. At age four, he made up his own compositions and studied violin. He insisted that all his activities be accompanied by music. His father noticed that it was difficult to teach him music — he seemed to know everything already. By the time he was five, he would stay up late, practicing by candlelight.

The next year, six-year-old Mozart went on tour, traveling by stagecoach all around the bumpy roads of Europe. (From all of his travels, Mozart eventually learned to speak fifteen languages.) He played for royalty, for the well-known musicians of the day, and in bars. At seven, he proposed marriage to Marie Antoinette (the future queen of France); at eight, he was composing symphonies; and at eleven, he composed his first opera. When composing, Mozart wore an apron to keep the ink off his clothes. He wore little velvet coats with lace ruffles and gold embroidery, and a little gold sword at his side.

He was known then as the most-kissed little boy in Europe. Today we think of him as the greatest musical prodigy who ever lived.

Mozart had a strange and exhausting childhood. He was so often ill that some people worried about how much longer he would live. He was sweet and affectionate, most anxious to please. His special talent meant he never had to go to school; his father gave him lessons. Mozart especially liked arithmetic and covered tablecloths and wallpaper with rows of figures.

Mozart loved animals. He sent the family dog, a terrier named Bimperl, greetings from cities all over Europe. In London, he broke off a concert to run after a cat that had wandered in. Later in life, he owned two other dogs (Goukerl and Katherl), a pet grasshopper, and various birds.

As a child Mozart was cute, with rosy cheeks and bright eyes. As an adult, though, his skin was yellowish, scarred from smallpox, and his blue eyes were bulgy. He was short and thin, and his head was too big for his body. Yet he was concerned about his appearance. He took care to have elegant clothes, and he had a barber work on his hair much more often than most people did.

Mozart fell madly in love with Aloysia Weber (cousin of composer Carl Maria von Weber), his landlady's daughter. But she rejected him, and he married Constanze Weber, her sister. Constanze was like Mozart in many ways: musical, not especially attractive (he called her "Little Mouse"), and playful. They had six children, but only two lived to adulthood.

Music was the one thing that made Mozart's face light up. He usually woke up at six, composed till nine, gave music lessons till one (though he didn't enjoy teaching), then had lunch at someone's house, where he had to entertain his hosts. Then, unless there was a concert to attend, he composed far into the night. He could get by on as little as four hours' sleep. Doctors told him he needed to get more regular recreation, which may be why he eventually bought a pool table.

He wrote music more quickly than almost any other composer in history, and he sometimes put things off till the very last minute. If he had to work through the night, Constanze would tell him tales about Cinderella or Aladdin to keep him awake.

His best ideas came when he was in a good mood, alone, and undisturbed. "What a delight this is I cannot tell!" he once wrote. "All this inventing, this producing, takes place in a pleasing, lively dream."

He could write down his ideas at meals (he liked liver dumplings and sauerkraut), while gossiping with friends, and even while playing pool. Once he held his wife's hand during childbirth and with his other hand wrote several pieces of music.

One day a visitor found Mozart and his wife dancing in their house, and Mozart explained that they had run out of firewood and were trying to stay warm. Mozart spent money faster than he could earn it, and he was always in debt. Part of the problem was that aristocrats paid him for music with things like watches and snuff boxes — not the cash that he needed to live on. (A letter that he wrote asking for a loan sold, two centuries later, for one hundred times the amount he had pleaded for.)

There were plenty of people who didn't like Mozart. They thought he was rude, immature, and irresponsible. One person who knew Mozart well said that she never heard him say one serious thing. He could be impatient with people who were not as bright as he was.

Although his father was always bombarding him with advice on how to make money and meet the "right" people, Mozart had trouble finding and keeping jobs. Once he lost a court appointment by being obnoxious and got himself literally kicked out of court. "There is the door; I will have nothing more to do with such a villain," said the man who fired him.

Mozart was scared of ghosts and loud noises, and he was superstitious, which explains his reaction to the tall, mysterious stranger who came to his house one night. Dressed all in gray, the stranger commissioned him to write a requiem (or funeral) mass.

The stranger would never give his name, but kept nagging Mozart to finish. Fearful, and convinced somehow that he was writing his *own* burial music, Mozart worked feverishly. Eventually the stranger was revealed to be a messenger from an eccentric count who had a habit of having well-known composers write something he could pass off as his own in private performances.

But by that time Mozart had died of kidney failure and malnutrition.

Mozart had spent fourteen years of his short life on the road, and he had never been very healthy. He was only thirty-five when he died. Some people feel that fear of the stranger hastened his death. Plays, operas, and movies have been written about the theory that he was poisoned by rival composer Antonio Salieri, but this rumor has never been proved.

At the peak of his career, Mozart earned as much money in one concert as his father earned in a year. Yet, at the time of his death, he owned very little. He had six coats (five red, his favorite color, and one white for court); three silver spoons; and 346 books. His most expensive possessions were his walnut piano and his pool table.

Musical Notes

♪ Mozart was unhappy with the way one of his singers responded when she was called on to shriek in the opera *Don Giovanni*. One day he crept up behind her and grabbed her at exactly the right moment. She gave him just the shriek he wanted.

♪ One of Mozart's most famous, lighthearted compositions is the string serenade *Eine kleine Nachtmusik* (*A Little Night Music*), written two months after his father died and as Mozart was recovering from a serious illness.

♪ The Piano Concerto no. 21 is now known as *Elvira Madigan* — not after a friend of Mozart's, but after a twentieth-century movie that used this as its theme song.

♪ More recordings of Mozart's music are bought today than recordings of any other composer's work.

♪ To play all of Mozart's music in a row would take 202 hours.

MOODINESS AND MOONLIGHT

LUDWIG VAN BEETHOVEN

BORN IN BONN, GERMANY, 1770
DIED IN VIENNA, AUSTRIA, 1827

German composer who was the dominant musical figure of the nineteenth century—particularly famous for his nine symphonies

MUSIC—NOT COOKING, GOOD MANNERS, OR FASHION— was Ludwig van Beethoven's whole life.

His father began giving him piano lessons before he was four years old. Young Beethoven was so small he had to stand on the piano bench in order to reach the keys; his father rapped his knuckles whenever he made a mistake. Neighbors recalled him as a tiny boy weeping in front of the piano. When he was a little older, his father roused Beethoven at midnight to show him off to friends he brought home from bars.

By the time he was twelve, Beethoven was an organist at court. He was already publishing music and earning a salary that kept his family going when his father, an alcoholic, could no longer take care of them. At age sixteen, he caught Mozart's attention: "Keep your eyes on him," the older composer is said to have urged people. "Someday he will give the world something to talk about."

Beethoven had a difficult childhood but he could be playful. One day he bet a church singer that he could throw him off stride by playing variations as he accompanied the singer on the organ during the service. The singer accepted the challenge, but Beethoven won the bet: The singer *was* distracted. And Beethoven *did* get in trouble.

Eventually, he became known as the greatest pianist of his time. He could play so beautifully that his listeners wept—and when they did, he would burst out laughing.

"You are fools!" he would say.

Yet if people talked while he played, he would stalk off in a huff. If he didn't like the audience, he wouldn't perform at all.

His talent and powerful personality attracted many friends, but his moodiness could make it hard to *stay* friends with him. He insulted everyone. For an overweight violinist, he wrote a song called "Praise to the Fat One." On his brother's business card—which read "Johann van Beethoven, Landowner"—Beethoven scrawled "Ludwig van Beethoven, Brain Owner."

Once he became angry with a prince who was important to his financial health, telling him, "There are and there will be thousands of princes. There is only one Beethoven."

A policeman arrested Beethoven one day for acting suspiciously. By this time the composer was very well known, and the policeman refused to believe that the "great Beethoven" could look as he did. The fashionable hairstyle of the day was careful pigtails, but Beethoven let his thick hair grow long and wild. He also couldn't be bothered with clean or stylish clothes. When his clothes became too dirty and disgusting, his friends took them away during the night and brought new ones. Beethoven never noticed the difference.

Even Beethoven admitted that he was not physically attractive: "I cannot love what is not beautiful—or I should be loving myself." He was short, with a huge head and hairy hands. His face was scarred from smallpox, and he had sad, nearsighted eyes. In later life, his ears were stuffed with pieces of cotton wool soaked in some yellow fluid. Only his protruding teeth were always clean: he constantly rubbed them with his napkin.

One of his favorite foods was macaroni and cheese. He also liked red herrings, a mushy soup of bread and eggs, and strong coffee that he made himself—exactly sixty beans to the cup. He was notorious for his bad cooking, and for his behavior in restaurants. Once he got so mad at a waiter that he dumped a plate of veal and gravy on the man's head—and laughed. He had a loud laugh and a loud, annoying voice. And he liked to spit. He sometimes left restaurants without paying and sometimes he wrote music on the bill.

"I am never alone when I am alone," Beethoven said. He usually got up early in the morning to compose, then later walked through the streets of Vienna, muttering, growling, and stamping his feet. He carried bulging notebooks of music with him at all times. His handwriting was so messy that almost no one other than himself could read it.

In the afternoon, he'd go to a coffeehouse to gossip and read the newspapers. Sometimes he worked all night, by moonlight, going without food or sleep. More to keep awake than to get clean, he would pour pitchers of water over his head, which annoyed his downstairs neighbors when the water flooded the floor and leaked through their ceiling. When a group of boys peeked in his ground-floor window one time, they caught him working in his underwear. His room was even more shocking: dirty laundry, half-eaten food, rusty pens, scribbled papers everywhere; there was even a full chamber pot under the piano. His landlords didn't like him, and he had to move once or twice a year.

Beethoven would have been difficult to live with. (One woman who rejected his proposal of marriage called him "ugly and half crazy.") He always had to have his own way. He never married, but he was always in love, often with a woman who was already married or engaged.

The saddest thing about Beethoven's life was his gradual deafness, beginning in his late twenties. But he was used to writing music he couldn't hear. As a child he had been too young to play the compositions he wrote. As his hearing grew worse and worse, he lived inside his head more than ever and kept on writing music with no loss of energy. He broke strings on his piano trying to pound loud enough so that he could hear the notes. Frustration made him more moody, even at times suicidal.

Beethoven conducting an orchestra was a sight to see. He would leap into the air during the loud parts, waving his arms toward the skies, sometimes shouting without being aware of it. Then he would crouch low during the quiet parts, almost creeping under the music stand. Audiences loved his music. In his last public performance, he began to cry when someone turned him around to make him aware of the roaring applause that he couldn't hear.

He died of liver failure at age fifty-seven. The legend is that he roused himself from his bed at the end during a violent thunderstorm and shook his fist at the sky, defiant as ever.

Mozart's *Requiem* (the same work Mozart had thought he was writing for his own funeral) was played at Beethoven's funeral. It was a sad day for Vienna: one out of ten people who lived there came to pay their respects.

Musical Notes

♪ Possibly the most famous notes of all time are the first four notes of Beethoven's Fifth Symphony — three short beats followed by one long beat. Some people think they represent the knocking of Fate at one's door.

♪ The last movement of Beethoven's Ninth Symphony is choral music set to Schiller's poem "Ode to Joy." The music has inspired people ever since it was written. It was played, for example, during the Chinese student protest in 1989, and when Germany's Berlin Wall came down in 1990.

♪ Beethoven dedicated the famous *Moonlight Sonata* to eighteen-year-old Countess Giulietta Guicciardi. He was in love with her — but he was also in a tight spot. He needed to take *back* another dedication he had made to her and give it to someone else.

♪ The famous piano piece called *Für Elise* may actually have been meant as *Für Therese* — a pupil who ended up refusing Beethoven's proposal of marriage.

Douze
pour le
Pianofort

"My Dear Corpse"

Frédéric Chopin

Born in Zelazowa Wola, Poland, 1810
Died in Paris, France, 1849

Polish composer of expressive music that established the piano as a solo instrument and has become the most frequently played piano music in history

EVEN AS A CHILD, Frédéric Chopin was terribly sensitive, almost not quite of this world. His family was musical, and baby Chopin would cry with pleasure at the beautiful sounds they could make.

The family pampered and adored him. He played dolls with his three sisters and went ice-skating with them. His first piano teacher was his older sister Louisa, age seven. With another sister, he started the *Literary Amusement Association* at age fourteen, a newspaper full of funny stories and daily events. (It was actually his diary.)

His life revolved around music. He started playing at age four and began performing at age eight (wondering what people thought about his velvet jacket perhaps more than what they thought about his music). He began publishing his own compositions in his teens. ("Hats off, gentlemen—a genius!" Robert Schumann, an older composer, wrote about Chopin.) Even his practical jokes were musical; he would put people to sleep with soft playing and then wake them with a bang.

Chopin also had deep feelings for Poland. When he left the country at age twenty, it is said that he took with him a silver cup full of Polish dirt. Much of the music he went on to write — the waltzes, mazurkas, polonaises — re-created feelings and sounds from his childhood in Poland.

People said that Chopin "looked like his music." He was pale, handsome, and unhealthy; he weighed less than a hundred pounds. His black, silky hair hung in locks on his forehead. He had a sweet smile and a big nose (he called it "huge"). He carried himself as proudly as a prince and never swore or was crude.

"He is no man, he is an angel, a god!" wrote one friend.

But he was not always so charming. Another friend called him "temperamental, full of fantasies, and unreliable." He was sometimes suspicious and self-centered, and his wit could be malicious. His feelings were easily hurt and he could spend a whole day sulking.

And he had some funny quirks. He couldn't sleep, for example, unless his slippers were lined up in front of the bed. He never entered a room left foot first. Sudden surprises — a servant coming into the room — made his hair stand on end. Some smells, such as cigarette smoke, made him sick, and he was too delicate to drink wine or coffee (he liked milk). He would only eat certain foods — bread, pastries, chicken, and fish. He had a horror of being buried alive and, on his deathbed, asked to be cut open before being buried.

Bach and Mozart were the only composers Chopin loved without reservation. Just before giving a concert, he would practice Bach. He wasn't crazy about other composers, and he wasn't a big reader, but all the famous musicians and writers of the time were his friends.

After being introduced to each other by composer Franz Liszt, Chopin and George Sand carried on one of the most famous love affairs of the nineteenth century. George Sand was a famous French novelist six years older than Chopin. Her real name was Aurore Dudevant, and she was an independent feminist who wore trousers, smoked cigars, wrote more than 60 novels and 19,000 letters, and, in her spare time, climbed mountains.

Chopin never married, but he and Sand lived in houses next door to each other in Paris. She called him "Chop" or "Chip-Chip," or sometimes "my dear corpse" or "my little complainer." He kept a lock of her hair in his diary till the day he died.

Their first vacation together they spent secretively, in a monastery on the island of Majorca. Chopin brought his volumes of Bach, some unfinished compositions, and plenty of music paper. He became sick and was coughing up blood by the time they returned. Later, spending summers at her house in the country, they had a quiet life — an early dinner outdoors, visits with friends. At twilight, Chopin would play for Sand. These were his most productive years.

Chopin got his ideas quickly, while walking or playing the piano. But he locked himself in his room for days at a time to perfect them — weeping, pacing like a madman, breaking pens. He could work for six weeks on a single page of music. Often he wrote in the middle of the night — he had a piano in his bedroom — much to the neighbors' bewilderment.

"He does not know on what planet he exists," said Sand of those times.

Chopin was one of the greatest pianists in history. His small, delicate hands — Sand called them "velvet fingers" — played softly but hypnotically. His feet were in constant motion, using the pedals so rapidly that his legs appeared to be vibrating. He hated large public performances, but the private concerts he held for friends became legendary.

One concert he played by moonlight, for a moth had fallen into the lamp and extinguished the flame.

To relieve the serious moods his playing evoked, he would break into imitations. He was an excellent mimic and some friends thought he should give up piano for acting. He never missed an opening night at the theater.

"I'm a revolutionary — money means nothing to me," Chopin said. Still, he didn't seem to mind having it. He supported himself by teaching five lessons a day, for which countesses, baronesses, and princesses paid well. They would enter his studio and place their money on the mantel while he looked out the window. (He thought a true gentleman didn't touch money.)

He lived in luxury. He had a servant, his own horse and carriage, and clothes from all the best shops: blue velvet coats, silk shirts, diamond stickpins, white leather gloves made to order, a flowing black cloak lined with gray satin. He liked to have vases of violets around his rooms, and even his handkerchiefs were perfumed.

Always sickly, Chopin died of tuberculosis at age thirty-nine — less than two years after he and Sand broke off their relationship. His last words were "Play Mozart in memory of me."

He was buried in Le Père Lachaise, a cemetery in Paris where many famous musicians are buried. The legend is that Chopin's silver cup of Polish dirt was poured on his grave.

Ever since, people say, not a day goes by without someone putting fresh flowers on Chopin's grave. He was a legend in his own time, and his compositions have never gone out of fashion.

Musical Notes

♪ The Waltz in D-flat was written for George Sand's dog. It's known as the "Minute Waltz" because it can be played in one minute. Chopin also wrote something known as the "Cat Waltz," supposedly inspired by the noise his cat made one day when it jumped on the piano.

♪ The song "Till the End of Time" was taken from a Chopin polonaise, for a movie about Chopin. It sold over a million records. "I'm Always Chasing Rainbows" is another popular American song whose melody comes from Chopin's work.

♪ The same singer sang at the funerals of Chopin, Beethoven, and Franz Joseph Haydn. Mozart's *Requiem* was played at Chopin's funeral, and so was Chopin's own *Funeral March,* which is one of the most famous funeral compositions ever written.

Aïda

A Successful Farmer and Opera Composer

Giuseppe Verdi

born in Le Roncole, Italy, 1813
died in Milan, Italy, 1901

Foremost Italian opera composer—melodies from his operas Aida, La Traviata, Rigoletto, *and* Il Trovatore *are familiar around the world*

On the day in 1814 when the army invaded the tiny Italian village of Le Roncole, Luigia Verdi ran up into the bell tower of the town's church. The soldiers killed everyone in the church except her and the baby she had grabbed on her way. They hid in the tower until the army was gone and it was safe to come down.

His mother had saved Giuseppe Verdi's life—and part of the history of opera.

As an altar boy at the same church a few years later, Verdi was so entranced when he first heard an organ play that he didn't hear the priest telling him what to do. The priest lost his temper and pushed the boy down the stairs. Verdi, when he came to, begged his parents for music lessons.

He was the village organist by age ten, and in his teens walked six miles, rain or shine, between two towns for his organist jobs. One stormy Christmas Eve, he fell into a flooded drainage ditch and had to be rescued.

Verdi married his childhood sweetheart, Margherita. He wrote his second opera during a tragic period when his wife and his two children fell ill and died. It was supposed to be a comic opera, but perhaps Verdi was too sad to make it lighthearted, for when it was produced the audience hissed their disapproval.

Verdi was disappointed and swore off composing. Then the manager of La Scala Opera House in Milan begged him to write music for a new libretto. Verdi wasn't going to read it, but his eye happened to fall on a page . . . and he was up all night. By morning he had the words memorized. The result was his third opera, *Nabucco,* and this time the roar of approval was so loud that Verdi was frightened — he thought the audience was booing.

With later operas, such as *Aida* and *La Traviata,* the rehearsal halls had to be sealed against thousands wanting early peeks. Verdi cared little what critics thought about his music, but he did want to please the public: "The public will stand for anything except boredom." The public was far from bored, and with his riches Verdi bought a farm in the country.

Verdi was probably the only important composer who was also a successful farmer. Using the latest techniques, he grew vegetables, raised livestock, and planted a tree every time he finished another opera.

He and his second wife, a famous soprano named Giuseppina, had no children. He loved animals and had cats, parrots, peacocks, and a spaniel named Loulou. He often wore a flower in his buttonhole and the only presents he liked were plants (especially cacti or palms).

Verdi liked the simple life. He awoke at five, walked around his estate, perhaps going for a sail across his lake in a small boat. He liked to read poetry (especially Shakespeare) and history, and he went to bed early.

Verdi might also be the only composer who was also a senator. With reluctance, he kept his appointment to the Italian legislature, where his main concern was to put free musical education in the schools.

Verdi would not have liked this book. He wanted his music to speak for him, and he thought his life was nobody's business. Once he hid out in a toolshed when a group of fans came to visit.

A much-loved figure in Italy, Verdi lived to be eighty-seven. His funeral was huge, and everyone sang songs from, of course, operas by Verdi.

Musical Notes

♪ The song "La Donna È Mobile," from *Rigoletto,* was kept from the tenor who was to sing it until the day before dress rehearsal. Verdi was afraid the song would get around and be whistled all over town once anyone heard it.

♪ At its premiere in Cairo, Egypt, in 1871, *Aida* starred live elephants as well as singers. Over one hundred years later, *Aida* is the most frequently performed opera at the Metropolitan Opera House in New York (with *La Traviata* and *Rigoletto* also in the top ten).

England
Wien
Paris

A Different White Dress Every Night

Clara Schumann

born in Leipzig, Germany, 1819
died in Frankfurt, Germany, 1896

German composer considered to be one of the greatest pianists of all time; a direct influence on the music of Robert Schumann and Johannes Brahms

WHEN CLARA WIECK WAS A LITTLE GIRL, a student of her father's used to tease her with scary stories. He would wait till the room got dark and then dress up as a ghost, making shapes in the dim light.

The man was Robert Schumann, and when Clara grew up, she married him.

Robert became a brilliant composer. But seeing Clara play at age nine was what gave him the idea of starting a career in music and studying with her father, one of the leading piano teachers in Germany.

Clara's childhood was most unusual. She could hardly talk and was at first thought to be a deaf-mute. Her father (her parents were divorced) started giving her piano lessons partly to reassure himself that she could hear. She began speaking normally at age eight . . . when she was already on her way to becoming a world-famous pianist.

Her concerts were so popular that police had to be called in to control crowds. Fancy desserts were named after her. Poets wrote poems about her. She was nervous before a concert, rarely satisfied with her performance, and often depressed afterward. But she found touring exhilarating and made dozens of tours outside Germany. In every town, she wore a different white dress each night.

Chopin called her "the only woman in Germany who can play my music," and Robert wrote all his music with her in mind. "Your eyes, you romantic girl," he once wrote, "follow me everywhere, and I often think one cannot make such music without a bride." He used some of her melodies, and she premiered his music, which was considered "weird," all over Europe.

She was the famous one during her marriage. She was known as Queen of the Piano, while he was known as Clara Wieck's husband. She was a much better pianist than he and could earn more in three weeks than he could in a year.

Clara Schumann composed some twenty-three piano works, and most of her concerts included at least one work of her own. But at age twenty she wrote: "I once thought that I possessed a creative talent, but I have given up that idea; a woman must not desire to be a composer, not one has done it, and why should I expect to?"

After she was married, she kept performing but stopped composing. Unable to practice whenever Robert was working, she practiced at night when he went out for a beer.

"There is not even one little hour in the whole day for myself!" she said. Besides teaching piano and organizing all the details of her concert tours, she supervised a household of three servants, spent several hours each day writing letters, nursed Robert through several breakdowns, and took care of her children — she had eight within sixteen years. She attributed her energy to the long walks she took each day.

Clara knew everybody: composers like Franz Liszt, Richard Wagner, and Felix Mendelssohn came to dinner. Her best friend was Johannes Brahms, fourteen years her junior. She inspired much of his music. "By rights," he wrote, "I should have to inscribe all my best melodies, 'Really by Clara Schumann.'"

She was left a widow at thirty-seven, when Robert died in an insane asylum. To support her family, she turned to performing full-time. She had a longer career than any man of the time — sixty years — and a larger repertoire.

Only arthritis stopped her performing. As she died, at age seventy-seven, she asked her grandson to play Robert's music for her. It was the last music she ever heard.

Musical Notes

♪ Three of Clara's daughters and several granddaughters became piano teachers, and many of her students became prominent teachers as well. One, Carl Friedberg, came to the United States and taught at what is now the Juilliard School of Music.

♪ During their first year of marriage, Robert composed more than 130 songs, his chief claim to fame. After their first child, he wrote three symphonies in rapid succession. Whenever Clara left on a tour, he was unable to compose.

♪ Robert wrote some of the best music there is for children learning to play piano — such as *Kinderszenen*, or *Scenes from Childhood*, and *Album for the Very Young* — because of his relationship with Clara when she was a child.

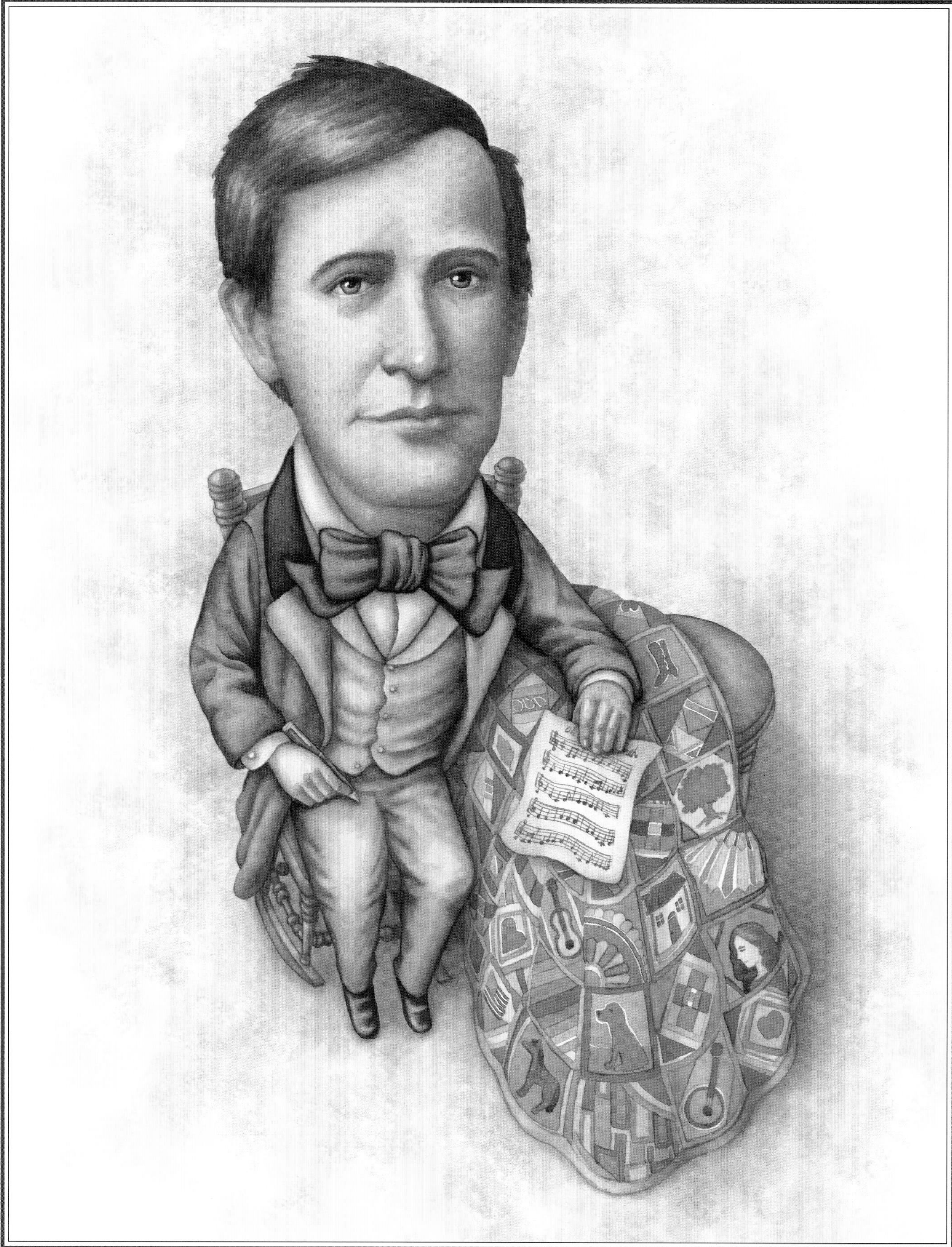

Stephen Foster

born in Lawrenceville, Pennsylvania, 1826
died in New York City, 1864

Creator of popular songs including "Beautiful Dreamer" and "My Old Kentucky Home"—often credited with being the first real American composer

IF YOU HAD ENTERED the Eagle Ice Cream Parlor in Pittsburgh, Pennsylvania, one day in 1847, you might have been part of the first public audience for a nonsense song called "Oh! Susanna." Within two years, it was the most popular song in America. Its author, Stephen Foster, was a twenty-one-year-old accountant.

Foster never got much money for the song. "Still," he said later, "the two fifty-dollar bills I received for it had the effect of starting me on my present vocation as a songwriter." They meant, for one thing, that he could stop working as an accountant.

Foster had a happy childhood and, as the youngest of ten, was used to being the center of attention. His family didn't think music was an appropriate activity for a boy. So he was mostly self-taught — picking out melodies on the guitar at age two, playing the flute at age seven. He wrote his first song at thirteen and would stay up late studying Bach and Mozart.

It was said that Foster couldn't sit down at the piano without playing a brand-new song, and his beautiful voice could bring tears to listeners' eyes. His father described his talent as "strange," but many of his songs, such as "Camptown Races," became so well loved that they're considered genuine American folk songs—people don't know who wrote them.

Foster's shy, gentle personality didn't change much after his success. He always looked melancholy and he could be stern. Once he asked a woman to decide on the spot between him and another man when both had arrived for a date at the same time. The woman, Jane McDowell, picked him—permanently. Their marriage wasn't always happy, and occasionally they separated. Their only child, Marion, grew up to become a music teacher.

Foster couldn't bear noise or interruption when he was composing. He spent days in his room. He didn't enjoy sports or exercise (except rambling around the woods near his home) and was sometimes too nervous to sleep.

He loved to read Edgar Allan Poe, and he took his daughter to theaters frequently, but he would leave in the middle if the music was poor.

Foster had simple tastes. He could make a meal of apples or turnips, using his pocketknife to peel them. He was a constant smoker.

Foster always spent more than he earned, and he never earned a great deal. Many people think his publishers cheated him.

The last year of his life was his most prolific; he had forty-six new songs published. Unfortunately, none of them were memorable, except for "Beautiful Dreamer" (said to be his last song). He could write a song in the morning, sell it in the afternoon, and spend the money in bars that night.

He frequently performed his "Hard Times Come Again No More" near the end of his life when he himself had fallen on hard times and was ill with tuberculosis.

One night while washing himself, he fainted and cut his throat on the wash basin. He was taken to the hospital, where he died, age thirty-eight. His worldly possessions consisted of some clothes and a purse.

The purse contained thirty-eight cents and a slip of paper on which Foster had written "Dear friends and gentle hearts"—probably the start of a new song.

Musical Notes

♪ "Jeanie with the Light Brown Hair" was one of many songs Foster wrote for his wife, Jane. Eighty-seven years later, in 1940–41, it was on early radio's "Hit Parade," and more people heard it than in all the years since it was created.

♪ George Gershwin's first hit song was "Swanee," probably picked up from Foster's "Swanee River," also known as "Old Folks at Home." When Foster's song, about a river in Florida, was published, he had never been farther south than the Ohio River. The legend is that he picked the name Swanee off a map. Today, "Swanee River" is the official state song of Florida, and Foster's "My Old Kentucky Home" is the official state song of Kentucky.

THE CHECKED COTTON UNDERWEAR OF

JOHANNES BRAHMS

BORN IN HAMBURG, GERMANY, 1833
DIED IN VIENNA, AUSTRIA, 1897

German composer who wrote masterpieces in almost every form except opera—most famous for his four symphonies and lush piano music

JOHANNES BRAHMS DID THINGS other people might have wished they could do. He fell asleep once when composer Franz Liszt was playing piano for him. He dressed strictly for comfort, and he left his clothes on the floor when he went to bed. He liked merry-go-rounds and circus sideshows. Not until he was almost thirty did he stop playing with tin soldiers.

Brahms had not always been able to do what he wanted. He grew up in the slums of Hamburg, surrounded by crime and disease.

His father, who was seventeen years younger than his mother, was a bass player who worked in bars. At an early age, Brahms helped support his family by playing dance music in waterfront bars. He kept a book propped up on the piano so he could read while he played, and when he got sleepy, bartenders plied him with drinks to keep him awake.

By the time he was fifteen, he was making a living through music. He left Hamburg to travel as an accompanist to a famous Hungarian violinist, carrying in his knapsack works of his own. Brahms was handsome when young, slender with long straw-blond hair, and he had a high voice that didn't change until he was twenty-four.

The foundation of his life was his friendship with Clara Schumann, who was fourteen years older than he was.

She advised him on matters large (she got jobs for him) and small (which slippers to take when he visited Hamburg), on things musical (she gave him piano lessons) and unmusical (how to invest his money; for a while he simply sent all of it to her). She did everything she could possibly do to help his career, and he wrote most of his music with her in mind.

He also gave two years of his life to helping Schumann and her children, with housekeeping, childcare, rearranging her library of books and music. (Brahms had a limited education, but he was a walking encyclopedia.) They wrote hundreds of letters to each other, some of which they later destroyed.

Brahms wasn't an instant success as a musician. At the first performance of a concerto on which he'd worked for four years, only three people clapped; everyone else hissed. But eventually his music became popular, and he was one of the few composers ever who didn't have to take another job to make a living.

He was one musician who spent less money than he earned. With his extra money, Brahms took care of relatives in Hamburg and any friend who needed help. His own tastes were simple in everything but music and food. He owned an expensive collection of original music manuscripts by Mozart and other composers he admired.

And Brahms loved food. The main melody of his Third Symphony came to him, he reported, after a meal of fresh asparagus and champagne. When a doctor told him he had to go on a diet, he protested that he was dining with composer Johann Strauss (one of his favorite dinner companions) that night — chicken with paprika! — and asked the doctor to pretend that he hadn't come to see him till the next day. Another much-loved dish was herring, and he adored eggnog. He would have three glasses of beer with dinner and always had coffee afterward.

His table manners were not the best. For breakfast he would eat sardines and drink the oil right from the tin.

Brahms lived for twenty-six years in the same apartment, and every day ate at the Red Hedgehog restaurant. Later in his life, people said that Brahms, with his short legs and the huge bushy beard that became his trademark, began to resemble a hedgehog himself.

"Before I had my beard, I looked like Clara Schumann's son," he said. "Now with it, I look like her father." A bashful man, he liked his beard because it "allows me to trot about so nice and anonymous."

He wore flannel shirts and short baggy pants that often showed several inches of checked cotton underwear. Another way you could catch a glimpse of his underwear was to watch him conduct an orchestra. He sometimes forgot to fasten his suspenders, and when he conducted, he'd have to grab his pants before they fell down.

He smoked cigars constantly and usually wore a shabby brown coat with cigar-ash smudges all over it. He walked the way Beethoven did, with his hands behind his back.

Brahms got up every morning at four or five, made his own coffee with his Viennese coffee maker, and went for a walk in the woods to hear the birds singing. He kept his pockets filled with candy and little pictures, which he handed to neighborhood children on his walks.

Then he would get to work. Brahms worked painstakingly. His first symphony took him about ten years to write. He prepared meticulous manuscripts, and if he wasn't completely satisfied with them he would burn them or throw the pages into the river. "It does not just come to you!" Brahms would say of composing. "It is torture!"

He often sought advice from friends, and he made friends easily. He wasn't a phony and couldn't tell even the smallest lie. Though he wasn't deceptive, he did work hard to charm: After an evening that Brahms spent drinking with Tchaikovsky, who hated him, Tchaikovsky grudgingly admitted that Brahms at least had "a nice sense of humor."

Brahms could be sarcastic and domineering, too. And very tactless: Once he was said to have excused himself from a dinner party by saying, "I beg a thousand pardons if there should be anyone here whom I have not insulted tonight!"

The one friend he never alienated was Schumann.

"Decorations mean nothing to me — I only want to have them." Brahms did have an ego. When he was passed over for a conducting job in Hamburg, he was bitter about it to the end of his life. He even blamed it for his failure to get married — "I would have become an orderly citizen," he mourned.

But Brahms never did marry. Perhaps he liked his freedom, perhaps other women paled next to Schumann, perhaps he had a fear of the unknown: "I cannot make up my mind to either a first opera or a first marriage," he liked to joke.

Brahms lived less than a year after Clara Schumann died. At age sixty-four, he died of cancer of the liver. All the ships in Hamburg lowered their flags to half-mast that day.

Musical Notes

♪ Brahms always slept like a baby. After all, he wrote "Brahms's Lullaby," also known as "Lullaby and Good Night," possibly the most famous lullaby ever. But no one could sleep in the same room with him — he was a notoriously loud snorer.

♪ Brahms is the third of the "Three *B*'s" — Bach, Beethoven, and Brahms. It was conductor Hans von Bülow who probably invented the term. He called Brahms's First Symphony "Beethoven's Tenth," meaning that Brahms's music was the logical next step after Beethoven's. The famous horn solo in this symphony was jotted down on a picture postcard Brahms sent to Clara Schumann from his summer home in the Tyrol.

♪ A survey of one hundred musicians taken in California in 1989 ranked Brahms as the number-one favorite composer.

Pulsing and Quivering

Peter Ilich Tchaikovsky

BORN IN VOTKINSK, RUSSIA, 1840
DIED IN ST. PETERSBURG, RUSSIA, 1893

The most popular nineteenth-century Russian composer, famous for ballets, symphonies, the 1812 Overture, *and the First Piano Concerto*

WAS THERE ANYONE EVER SO UNHAPPY AS PETER TCHAIKOVSKY?

As a baby, he constantly drummed on windowpanes, tapping out melodies. One day he tapped too hard, broke the glass, and badly cut his hand. At age seven, after hearing Mozart's *Don Giovanni* on a music box, he begged for piano lessons. But playing the piano made him too excited to sleep.

His father didn't think music was a fit career, so Tchaikovsky became a law clerk. The separation from his mother when he was sent away to law school crushed him. One month after her death, he was writing his first music.

He got musical ideas quickly: "I forget everything and behave like one demented. Everything inside me begins to pulse and quiver." Writing music, he felt, was the only thing that redeemed him from worthlessness.

Tchaikovsky gave away half of any money he received and spent the rest. He had expensive tastes — in transportation (he always took cabs), food, wine, cigarettes (he smoked constantly), and perfumes. He was a handsome "man about town." He dressed impeccably, down to his white gloves and cane. When he didn't want to be recognized he wore huge dark glasses. He liked to play cards, especially whist and solitaire.

Though Tchaikovsky frequently had houseguests, he lived quietly. He rose at eight and had strong tea with lemon. When composing, Tchaikovsky would forget to sleep and eat — or maybe he thought of his music as food. Once, in the middle of a song-writing frenzy, he wrote, "I continue to bake musical pancakes." The last country house he lived in was very private and was surrounded by flower beds. It had a grand piano with a seven-foot couch nearby where he could rest.

Tchaikovsky had constant headaches and indigestion. He always thought he was about to die. One night he burned all the volumes of his diary when he realized that when he died people would know his secrets.

His most nerve-racking time was when he had to conduct an orchestra: He was terrified of literally losing his head while conducting. So he would hold on to it with his left hand while beating time with his right.

Tchaikovsky was involved in two strange relationships. He married a woman

who said she would kill herself if he didn't marry her. She had a habit of biting her nails till her fingers bled—her letters to him were spotted with blood. After nine weeks of marriage, he himself tried to commit suicide by diving into an icy river.

He survived, and that same year began a long friendship with a mysterious rich widow nine years older than he was. With the condition that they never meet, she offered to send him whatever money he needed. A few times they ran into each other by accident but both of them turned red and fled.

When she abruptly broke off correspondence without explanation, he was distraught. He died three years later at age fifty-three, mumbling her name.

There are two stories about Tchaikovsky's death. Some say he carelessly drank unboiled water during a cholera epidemic, contracting the fatal disease. Others think he took poison because he was being blackmailed. Tchaikovsky was homosexual at a time when this was considered completely unacceptable socially, and members of the aristocracy were said to be threatening to expose him unless he killed himself.

He died within ten days of the premiere of his Sixth Symphony, the *Pathétique*, which he considered his best work.

Musical Notes

♪ It is said that *The Nutcracker Suite* (six selections from *The Nutcracker* ballet by Tchaikovsky) has gotten more people interested in classical music than any music in history. It is one of the most recorded works ever. Many ballet dancers, including Margot Fonteyn, started their careers with roles in this ballet.

♪ The noisy *1812 Overture,* celebrating the retreat of Napoleon's troops from Moscow, was not performed in the Soviet Union the way Tchaikovsky intended—outdoors, with the ringing of church bells, live cannon fire, and fireworks—until 1990.

♪ Tchaikovsky was the conductor at the opening night of Carnegie Hall in New York City, in 1891. But Tchaikovsky was unhappy there, too—he cried all the time in his hotel room.

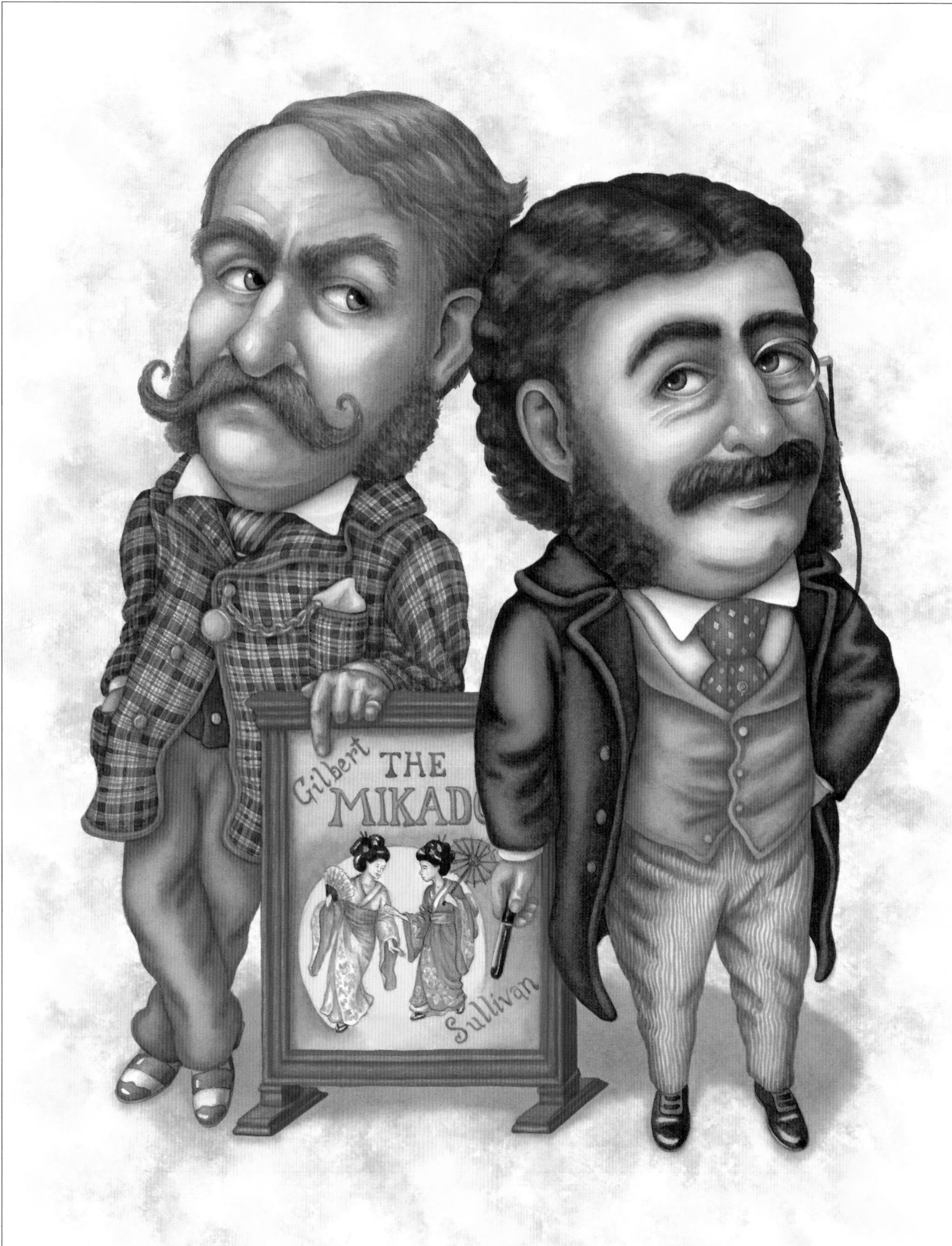
Gilbert
THE
MIKADO
Sullivan

TOPSY-TURVYDOM

GILBERT & SULLIVAN

BORN IN LONDON, ENGLAND, 1836; DIED IN HARROW WEALD, ENGLAND, 1911 *(Gilbert)*
BORN IN LONDON, ENGLAND, 1842; DIED IN LONDON, ENGLAND, 1900 *(Sullivan)*

An English humorist (Gilbert) and a composer (Sullivan) who together wrote comic operas such as The Mikado, H.M.S. Pinafore, *and* The Pirates of Penzance

SIR WILLIAM GILBERT AND SIR ARTHUR SULLIVAN were not friends. But somehow, mostly by correspondence, they collaborated for twenty years on fourteen operettas.

Gilbert wrote the words. He was the tall one, grouchy and a bit sloppy. He said something funny every time he opened his mouth. He quarreled with everyone and was frequently in court, suing people. Once he drew a picture of himself saying "I like pinching little babies." His kind of humor was very different from the proper style of the times. He called it "topsy-turvydom": "Where vice is virtue — virtue, vice; / Where nice is nasty — nasty, nice."

Sullivan wrote the music. He was the short, charming one — a born showman.

Gilbert married a woman he called "Kitten" (her name was Lucy). She published *Kitty's Cookery Book,* a collection of recipes. They had no children, but had pets (ordinary ones, as well as monkeys, parrots who could swear, turkeys, and a bee named Buzfuz) that they treated like people: each pet had its own bed and its own toys.

Sullivan dated several glamorous women but never married.

Sullivan kept twenty volumes of diaries so personal he had brass locks for them. He loved Shakespeare. He liked fancy food. He hung around with royalty at garden parties and was so sociable that he could compose with people around him. He smoked endless cigarettes and he had expensive tastes — gambling, yachting, and racehorses.

Gilbert kept few diaries. He hated Shakespeare. He liked plain food — steak pie, cold boiled beef, cheese, and beer. He spent his days writing, coaching rehearsals, and playing tennis. He needed peace and quiet.

Gilbert and Sullivan last met when they took a bow together at their final operetta. They came on stage from different directions and wouldn't speak to each other.

Sullivan died of bronchitis at age fifty-eight. The last words in his diary were "I am sorry to leave such a lovely day."

"A Gilbert is no good without a Sullivan," Gilbert said after Sullivan's death. He died eleven years later, at age seventy-four. He dived into his lake to save a woman friend from drowning and had a heart attack.

What did Gilbert and Sullivan have in common? First, a strong sense of humor.

"I was screaming with laughter the whole time," said Sullivan about the first script Gilbert brought him *(Trial by Jury)*. "We always saw eye to eye," Gilbert once said about their reactions to jokes.

Both worked hard. Sullivan said that "musical composition, like everything else, is the outcome of hard work. . . . If I had waited for inspiration I am afraid I should have done nothing." They were perfectionists about their works on stage, planning every detail. Gilbert was known as a tyrant with the actors; he could swear for five minutes straight without repeating himself.

The operettas made them both rich. Gilbert's last house was in the country, staffed by forty servants, and surrounded by one hundred acres of farmland and a private lake. He drove a Rolls-Royce. Sullivan lived in a luxurious apartment near Westminster Abbey.

Mostly what they had in common was their work—operettas that poked fun at English government, art, and fashions. And, because of the special Gilbert and Sullivan combination of the wise and the silly, even people who have never been to England have been royally entertained ever since.

♪ Although Sullivan was the most successful serious English composer of his time, his only work remembered now (besides the operettas) is the hymn "Onward Christian Soldiers."

♪ When he was two, Gilbert was kidnapped and held for ransom in Italy. He never forgot the experience, and it later inspired the plot of *The Gondoliers*.

♪ Gilbert got the idea for *The Mikado* when, after a fight with Sullivan, he was pacing in his study and a huge Japanese sword on the wall suddenly crashed to the floor. He had to rewrite the plot eleven times, but this turned out to be the most successful English opera ever written.

♪ *H.M.S. Pinafore* was another huge success. It was performed so frequently that at one time almost every child in England and America could sing its tunes.

Velvet Gentleman

Erik Satie

born in Honfleur, France, 1866
died in Paris, France, 1925

Influential French composer famous for simple and elegant piano music with bizarre titles

HE WAS BORN ERIC SATIE, but by the time he first composed music, he had changed the spelling of his name to Erik. No one knows why.

About his childhood, he said he "was born very young into a world very old." (He lived with his grandparents.) An eccentric uncle influenced him, and so did the stepmother he hated—she composed popular piano waltzes. Satie, a lazy student, got kicked out of music school. He went back to school at age forty. All his life, he read fairy tales, animal stories, and *Alice's Adventures in Wonderland.*

Satie's imagination was unlike any other musician's. His *Parade,* an experimental ballet, provoked a riot with its ragtime rhythms and sound effects. He wrote "Flabby Preludes (For a Dog)," "Sketches and Exasperations of a Big Boob Made of Wood," and "Waltz of the Mysterious Kiss in the Eye."

Satie also put whimsical instructions in his works, from "Like a nightingale having a toothache" to "Don't frown." "Sports and Diversions" has an "Unappetizing Chorale" ("composed on an empty stomach") that reads, "I dedicate this chorale to those who do not like me—and withdraw."

Satie's second favorite form of communication after music was letters. Mostly his letters were witty, though once they almost landed him in jail for slander.

He became known as the Velvet Gentleman because he always wore gray velvet-corduroy jackets and carried a black velvet umbrella. He cut a dignified figure . . . except when overcome by unexpected fits of laughter. He had a deep, drawling voice and made entertaining conversation.

Satie never married: "I am a man whom women do not understand." His only love affair was with Suzanne Valadon, an artist who is now most famous for being the mother of the painter Maurice Utrillo. Her first painting was a picture of Satie. (Many artists of the time, including Pablo Picasso, drew Satie's portrait.) Satie said he liked the way she belched. They spent days sailing toy boats in the ponds at the park, and he bought her necklaces of sausages.

For most of his life, Satie lived in one room over a cafe in a shabby neighborhood. Every day he walked six miles to the bars where he played piano. In the

middle of the night he'd walk back, a hammer in his pocket for protection, jotting down musical ideas on street corners. His beautiful handwriting and many doodles made his manuscripts works of art.

Satie had the nickname of "Mr. Poverty" and made a point of being poor: "I have never been success oriented, and I hope that I never will be." He believed a person should sacrifice for art. Friends helped out, though he once remarked, "It's odd. You find people in every bar willing to offer you a drink. No one ever dreams of presenting you with a sandwich."

He died of cirrhosis of the liver at age fifty-nine.

When his brother went to his apartment after Satie's death, he was the first stranger there in twenty-seven years. The room reminded people of an immense spiderweb. One of the two pianos was buried under newspapers. There was gymnastic equipment, but no bed, just a hammock.

And there were twelve velvet suits, six of them unworn, and 200 umbrellas.

♪ Satie invented "wallpaper music," or background music meant *not* to be listened to, like the music in elevators today. He composed the first film music, for the film that was part of his ballet *Relâche.* He also starred in the film. On the curtain in the theater was written: "Erik Satie is the greatest musician in the world; whoever disagrees with this notion will please leave the hall."

♪ To escape from the military, Satie stood outside bare-chested one winter night, caught severe bronchitis, and spent three months in bed. There he wrote three *Gymnopédies,* the Greek dances that are still his most famous work.

♪ In New York in 1963, the world's record for the longest musical piece ever played was set — Satie's *Vexations* (to be played 840 times in a row). It took eighteen hours.

♪ Modern composer Philip Glass's first concert featured *Music in the Form of a Square,* a play on Satie's *Three Pieces in the Shape of a Pear,* which were actually *seven* pieces he wrote after composer Claude Debussy accused his music of being too shapeless. Satie influenced other contemporary composers such as John Cage, Terry Riley, Steve Reich, and William Ackerman, who founded Windham Hill Records.

MAPLE LEAF RAG

THE ENTERTAINER

SCOTT JOPLIN

BORN IN TEXARKANA, TEXAS, 1868
DIED IN NEW YORK CITY, 1917

Pulitzer Prize–winning American pianist and composer considered the father of ragtime, which has influenced African-American music ever since

SCOTT JOPLIN'S FATHER, who played fiddle as a hobby, didn't know any black men who made a respectable living from music. But Scott Joplin's mother, who played banjo as a hobby, was sure her son was destined for a musical career. She dusted around him while he played songs by Stephen Foster on the piano at a house where she cleaned. She worked hard to pay for his piano lessons until area music teachers started offering to teach Scott Joplin for free.

While other boys his age partied, Joplin practiced hard. He probably didn't go to school until his teens, because of the scarcity of schools for black children. A favorite book was *Alice's Adventures in Wonderland.*

He left home at age seventeen and began playing piano in bars. The Silver Dollar Saloon in St. Louis drew Joplin for seven years. It was like a college where he learned about music until he went to a real college, at age twenty-eight. Every time he returned to St. Louis, Joplin was greeted with a parade.

In the clubs where Joplin played, the air would be thick with smoke, and the room filled with pool tables and a bar. Hanging gas lamps would shed little light toward the piano, and usually people talked so loud you couldn't hear the music anyway . . . except on the nights when Scott Joplin, advertised as "The Entertainer," played.

Joplin published many of his own pieces, fifty in all, with John Stark, a white publisher, in a cross-race friendship unusual for the times. After the enormous success of his most famous piece, "Maple Leaf Rag," Joplin spent long hours shut up in his study, working at an oak rolltop desk.

He wrote a ballet called *The Ragtime Dance* and an opera called *A Guest of Honor.* The first was published but was a complete commercial failure.

The second has never been found. Once he left a trunk full of his possessions with his landlady in Baltimore, saying he'd be back for it when he could pay her. The trunk, which may have held the only copy of *A Guest of Honor,* has never turned up.

Joplin was married twice, first to Belle Hayden. Their only child, a daughter, died as a baby, and the pair separated soon after. Parties in the apartments where Joplin lived in New York with his second wife, Lottie Stokes, were full of good food and music. He liked beer and gambling. He rarely spoke in a voice louder than a whisper, but he had a magnetic personality. Younger pianists idolized him, and he helped many of them out.

Believing in himself even in the face of the indifference of the public, Joplin kept working on his second opera, *Treemonisha.* He burned some unfinished works, including a symphony. He wanted to make it with opera or not make it at all.

But *Treemonisha* failed. The one performance he was able to mount, in Harlem in 1915, was ignored. There were no reviews, good or bad. Within two years, Joplin died at age forty-nine, from advanced syphilis. He was buried on Long Island in an unmarked grave.

Over fifty years later, albums of Scott Joplin music represented 74 percent of the top-selling classical recordings. The second performance of *Treemonisha* took place fifty-seven years after the first, at the Atlanta Symphony Hall in 1972. Considered the first truly American opera, it was awarded the Pulitzer Prize in music in 1976.

Joplin's gravestone now reads "Scott Joplin, American Composer."

Musical Notes

♪ The bouncy, syncopated rhythm known as ragtime was called "ragged time" at first, because it sounded as ragged as a torn piece of cloth. People who didn't like ragtime music said it was an addictive poison that caused permanent brain damage and ruined people's morals.

♪ "Maple Leaf Rag," published in 1899, was the first piece of sheet music to sell more than one million copies.

♪ Joplin became concerned about the way others were playing ragtime and started having a notice printed on his music: "Notice! Do not play this piece fast. It is never right to play 'Ragtime' fast. Author."

♪ Film director George Roy Hill used Joplin's music in his 1974 movie *The Sting*. After the film won Academy Awards for Best Picture, Best Score, and Best Title Song, interest in ragtime reached a new high.

Mutual
Life

HE STRETCHED OUR EARS

CHARLES IVES

BORN IN DANBURY, CONNECTICUT, 1874
DIED IN NEW YORK CITY, 1954

Modern American composer famous for unconventional piano works and symphonies, one of which, the Third Symphony, won the Pulitzer Prize

THE NEW ENGLAND CHILDHOOD of Charles Ives meant so much to him that he refused to visit his hometown later — he couldn't bear to see the changes that had taken place.

Ives worshiped his father, a bandleader, who was always trying to "stretch Ives's ears" with unusual sounds. Ives started learning piano, cornet, and violin at age five, and later the drums (the neighbors complained). At thirteen, he was the youngest church organist in Connecticut. On Saturdays he played ragtime piano in bars.

Sometimes his interest in music confused him. What was he doing inside while other kids were playing outside? So he went out for sports — track and tennis, football and baseball — and excelled at these, too.

Except as a church organist, Ives never earned money from music. He was a New York businessman and ran a highly successful insurance company.

Most people at work had no idea of his secret life: each evening he rushed home and wrote music that re-created the sounds of his Yankee childhood.

Ives married a woman named Harmony, who, despite her musical name, was a registered nurse. They adopted a daughter, Edith. Edith was allowed to play with her dolls under the piano while Ives composed, as long as she was quiet. The family had a horse, a dog, and a cat, Christofina, who ate asparagus.

Summers were spent in the country, in a spacious house full of books, surrounded by hills. Ives kept his old baseball cap in his studio, and also pictures of his father and Abraham Lincoln.

When Ives's music started becoming better known, he didn't seem to mind its unpopularity: "I'm the only one, with the exception of Mrs. Ives and one or two others perhaps . . . who likes any of my music."

Ives had a heart attack, the first of several, at age thirty-two and began to live as a recluse. He wrote his music in pencil with such a shaky hand that almost no one could read his writing.

He had a photographic memory of everything he'd written — all ten drawersful of messy manuscripts in his barn.

Ives did not own a radio or record player, rarely used the phone, and would yell at airplane pilots from the ground. He shunned publicity — a *Life* magazine photographer said he had never seen a person so terrified of the camera.

He wore old soft shirts, old pants, a battered brown felt hat, and an old corduroy

jacket. He drove a Model T and was a wild driver. An apple-pie American, he liked to write letters to the president suggesting amendments to the constitution.

When Ives felt sad, he would play "Onward Christian Soldiers" until he felt better. When he felt happy, he sang a nonsense song about codfish hanging in the sky. In the evenings, he would sit before the fire, and Mrs. Ives would read aloud for several hours from Charles Dickens and Jane Austen.

Ives liked iced tea and roast pork. He wasn't supposed to eat sweets but sometimes did anyway, and the milk he was supposed to drink he threw out in the backyard when people weren't looking.

After he was awarded the Pulitzer Prize in music, he gave away the money. "Prizes are for boys — I'm grown up!" he explained.

Ives had his final heart attack at age seventy-nine. One of his uncompleted works was the *Universe Symphony,* meant to be performed outdoors, by orchestras on the tops of several hills.

♪ Ives's orchestral works are said to be the most difficult composed by any composer anywhere. Hardly any of his music was performed during his lifetime, but by 1976, he was the modern American composer most frequently heard in orchestral performances.

♪ Ives's favorite piece of his own music was the "Fourth of July" part of his *Holidays Symphony*. It has the sounds of a small-town celebration — women unloading picnic baskets, fireworks, political discussions, and competing marching bands.

♪ The *Concord Sonata,* his best-known piano work, has sections named after the New England writers Ives loved: Ralph Waldo Emerson, Nathaniel Hawthorne, the Alcotts (Bronson and Louisa May), and Henry David Thoreau. This work is so difficult that Ives wrote a book to go along with it, called *Essays Before a Sonata.*

♪ Ives was an enthusiastic borrower. Old hymns, cowboy songs, Christmas carols, Stephen Foster melodies, African-American music, and the theme from Beethoven's Fifth Symphony can be found in his work — all used in new ways.

Standing on His Head

Igor Stravinsky

Born in Oranienbaum, Russia, 1882
Died in New York City, 1971

Russian-American composer widely considered the most influential of the twentieth century, most famous for the ballets Petrushka, The Firebird, *and* The Rite of Spring

THE MOST FAMOUS RIOT in classical music history took place on May 29, 1913, at the Paris premiere of *The Rite of Spring.* Half the people stood up and cheered; the other half screamed till their faces turned purple. Police arrived to break up fights. Hardly a note of the music could even be heard.

Igor Stravinsky, who had written the music, left the theater and took a taxi to a park. "I have never again been that angry," he said.

The most wonderful event of the year to Stravinsky when he was a child was the coming of spring: "The violent Russian spring that seemed to begin in an hour and was like the whole earth cracking."

Otherwise, said Stravinsky, "I do not like to remember my childhood."

His father, an opera singer, had an uncontrollable temper, and Stravinsky was frightened of him. Nor was he close to his mother (even after he was famous, she could scold him until he almost cried for not writing music like the composers *she* liked), or his piano teacher (a "blockhead").

Stravinsky saw Tchaikovsky's *The Sleeping Beauty* at age eight, started piano

lessons, and was soon spending six nights a week at the theater. Later, his parents insisted that he go to law school, but encouragement from his music teacher gave Stravinsky the idea of leaving law for music.

Stravinsky was one of very few composers who reached success overnight, in his case with *The Firebird,* a ballet based on old Russian legends. And after *The Rite of Spring,* which some say changed the whole course of music, he was world famous for the rest of his life. He developed self-confidence and a large ego. To amuse himself, he kept a file of pictures of conductors in ridiculous poses.

Stravinsky supported himself through composing. When asked about the high fees he charged, he explained, "I do it on behalf of my brother composers, Schubert and Mozart, who died in poverty."

Always in search of the quiet he needed to compose, Stravinsky left Russia for Switzerland, then Paris, and finally California, where he lived in Hollywood. He married his cousin and childhood sweetheart, Catherine Nosenko. One of their four children, Soulima, was a pianist who later toured with his father. After Catherine died, Stravinsky married Vera Sudeikin, a painter.

"My music is best understood by children and animals," Stravinsky claimed.

When in a new city, he always visited the zoo first. He smoked cigarettes in a long holder made of an albatross beak. His house was full of birds.

His work habits were compulsively neat. His writing desk had carefully arranged erasers, bottles of five different colored inks, glittering steel rulers, writing instruments (some of his own invention), and a pile of dictionaries (he knew four languages).

When lunch — perhaps rare roast beef, dark bread, and Italian espresso — was ready, Mrs. Stravinsky would clap her hands in the hall beneath his studio. If he was ready, he would clap his hands, too.

He relaxed by playing card games, going to movies, standing on his head (he said it cleared his brain), and sunbathing nude. He wore a battered green beret, even to bed, and had a vast collection of silk scarves. Superstitious, he wore sacred medals pinned to his underwear.

Stravinsky had many illnesses, including tuberculosis. But he must have been stronger than he seemed, because he lived until he was eighty-nine. He is buried in the Russian corner of an Italian cemetery.

Musical Notes

♪ In 1940, Stravinsky was the only living composer whose music was used in Walt Disney's movie *Fantasia. The Rite of Spring* accompanies animated scenes of erupting volcanoes, prehistoric forests, and battling dinosaurs.

♪ Stravinsky liked challenges and was always accepting difficult commissions. He once wrote a piece called "Do Not Throw Paper Towels in Toilet" and also wrote a polka for fifty elephants wearing ballet tutus.

♪ Stravinsky was one of the few composers whose complete works were recorded mostly under his own supervision — thus leaving a guide to how he wished his music to be played.

Tender Tyrant

Nadia Boulanger

born in Paris, France, 1887
died in Paris, France, 1979

French composer and conductor,
famous as the most influential music teacher of the twentieth century,
who guided several generations of American composers

As a baby Nadia Boulanger hated music — it made her cry or hide under the piano. "What a strange little girl we have!" her father would say. Then, at age three, she heard a fire siren outside the apartment, went to the piano to re-create the sound, and stayed at one piano or another for the next eighty-nine years.

Boulanger's first music teacher was her mother, a former Russian princess who was strict and a perfectionist. To force her to develop good posture, she tied Boulanger to chairs when she was a baby; all her life Boulanger walked somewhat stiffly. By age thirteen, Boulanger was performing on the organ and piano, and at seventeen she began teaching, supervising her younger sister Lili's education.

Lili became a brilliant composer, the first woman to win the Prix de Rome — an important prize in music composition. When Lili died at age twenty-four, Nadia — who got only as far as a second-place Prix de Rome — gave up her own composing and concentrated on teaching to support herself and her mother.

Women at that time in France were, by law, paid half as much as men doing the same work. Boulanger got around this by deciding to work twice as hard.

Her classes and private lessons became legendary. She had a gift for making things she had said many times sound spontaneous and for giving each pupil close attention. "As a teacher," she said, "my whole life is based on understanding others, not on making them understand me." People started coming to her from all over the world.

She had two grand pianos and one organ in rooms filled with fresh flowers. Over the fireplace was a white marble bust of her sister, Lili, and everywhere there were gifts from musician friends and thousands of music books covered in brown paper. In her bathroom was a giant metal bathtub you had to climb a ladder to enter.

Boulanger dressed and acted to look older than she was. She carried a big black leather satchel full of music, which students would vie to carry. She seldom smiled, but had expressive hands that could show any emotion. She wore a flowery perfume and adored exotic bath oils.

Nicknamed the "Tender Tyrant," Boulanger was not always popular. After group class, students emerged so drained that they would file across the street to a cafe

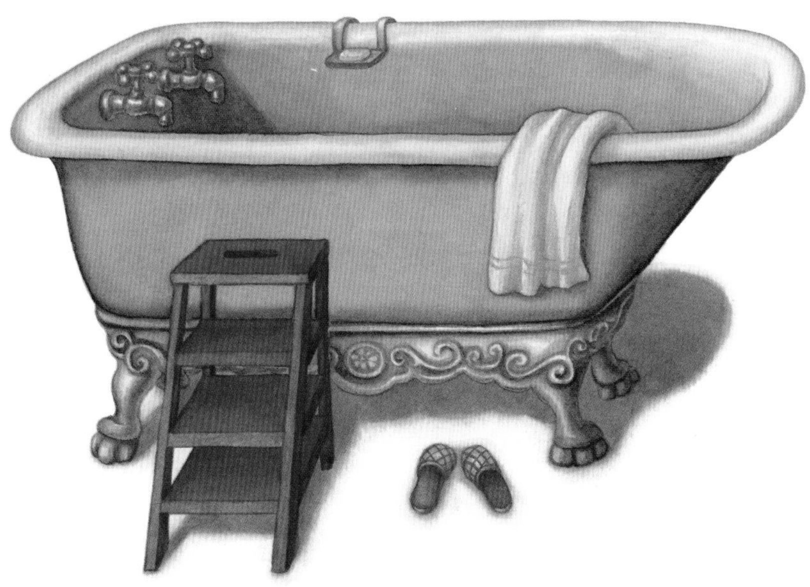

for coffee or beer, sitting in silence, not even saying good-bye when they left. One student recalls her saying only one nice thing to him in two whole years of study. On occasion, she would ridicule students and make them cry.

She ate lunch during lessons, and pupils worried about whether her plate would slide onto the piano keys. Between lessons, she ate yogurt or took catnaps. She stayed up late writing letters—she wrote thousands each year. Every New Year's she gave a costume ball, with lavish food, to which she invited her many famous friends.

With electrifying energy, she worked well into her eighties, teaching, traveling, and touring. She never married. She didn't believe marriage and a career in the arts were compatible.

Boulanger loved rich food and wouldn't stop eating it even when she lost her teeth—she swallowed chunks of food without chewing. She died at age ninety-two of a stomach blockage.

Her own music was played at her funeral, along with music by Bach and Lili Boulanger.

Musical Notes

♪ Boulanger's music students included pianist Dinu Lipatti, violinist Yehudi Menuhin, and composers Leonard Bernstein, Joe Raposi (creator of the Muppets' music), Aaron Copland, Philip Glass, Thea Musgrave, Quincy Jones, Virgil Thomson, and many others.

♪ In numerous cities Boulanger was the first woman to conduct a symphony orchestra, and she premiered many important works. She didn't like being singled out because she was a woman. "I've been a woman for a little over fifty years," she said when asked how she felt about being the first woman to conduct the Boston Symphony, "and have gotten over my initial astonishment."

♪ Boulanger believed that music has a moral purpose in the world, and that it was crucial for a student to be passionate about it. She would advise her students: "Do not take up music unless you would rather die than not do so."

The Ugly Duckling
and Juliet

Full of Splinters

Sergei Prokofiev

born in Sontsovka, Ukraine, 1891
died in Moscow, Soviet Union, 1953

Russian composer known for concertos, operas, symphonies, film music, ballet scores, and his famous work for children, Peter and the Wolf

SERGEI PROKOFIEV HEARD MUSIC even before he was born. His mother, while pregnant, played the piano for hours each day, especially Chopin and Beethoven.

As a child, Prokofiev never wanted to be anything other than a composer. After (like Stravinsky) seeing Tchaikovsky's *The Sleeping Beauty* at age eight, he wrote his first opera—*The Giant.* When he wasn't composing "puppies" (what he called his early pieces), he played with tin soldiers and dolls, built the dollhouses himself, and went walking on stilts.

Prokofiev rarely smiled and was not popular. He always had to say what he thought. If someone said, "It's a pleasure to meet you," he might growl back, "On my part there is no pleasure." When he was a student, he kept a chart of mistakes that other students made in class. He himself admitted that he was "full of splinters."

Nor was his music popular at first. Critics got so used to jumping on him that one once published a bad review of a piece that was never performed. They even picked on his appearance: "He looks like the fourth from his *Love for Three Oranges.*"

His violent piano playing startled audiences. Some people said that the way he attacked the piano made them think of trees being uprooted. He had long, dangly arms and huge hands that were always moving over an invisible keyboard, even when he slept.

But Prokofiev never gave up. If people walked out during his concerts, he blamed them, not the music. In America, he spent hours gazing at the skyscrapers around Central Park in New York, furious at "the wonderful American orchestras that cared nothing for my music."

Prokofiev married twice, once to Lina Llubera, a Spanish singer with whom he had two sons, and later to Myra Mendelson, a Russian writer.

He could work fourteen hours a day, not stopping except to eat or to tell his children to be quiet. He wrote so much music that he tended to forget his own compositions. He'd hear a piece he liked on the radio . . . and then realize he wrote it.

Prokofiev was unpopular even as a neighbor. He was once evicted when his downstairs neighbor accused him of playing the same "barbaric" chord on the piano 218 times in a row.

He always dressed carefully. He wore a jacket and tie to breakfast. He was fond of a bright red dressing gown and loved perfume. He would walk for miles in any weather to buy cigarettes and he'd give the colored cigarette boxes to children on his walks.

He had a wolflike dog named Mendoza, and a cat who liked to sleep in his favorite armchair.

Prokofiev might have liked this book. He loved biographies of musicians. He himself kept a diary, which he wrote in even while in the bathroom, and notebooks containing all his reviews (even the bad ones) and notes on his chess games. Next to music, he loved best to play chess and was an excellent player.

His final opera, *A Tale of a Real Man,* was banned by Russian leader Joseph Stalin for political reasons and was never produced during Prokofiev's lifetime. When Prokofiev died of a stroke at age sixty, his death went unreported for a week, because Stalin had died on the same day.

Musical Notes

♪ When it was first composed, much of Prokofiev's music was so controversial that conductors of his symphonies sometimes received death threats. Today he is one of the most frequently performed modern composers.

♪ *Peter and the Wolf* demonstrates the various instruments of the orchestra at the same time as it tells a story. Among the many famous narrators of the story was Prokofiev himself. He called this work "a present not only to the children of Moscow, but also to my own." Children around the world have been introduced to classical music by way of *Peter* ever since.

♪ As a child at the piano, Prokofiev left out the black keys when he played because they frightened him. Even in his twenties, he wrote "white" music, to be played entirely on white keys.

♪ The first four notes of his First Piano Concerto were nicknamed "hit on the head" because they sound so powerful.

PORGY
and BESS

"Great, Isn't It?"

George Gershwin

Born in Brooklyn, New York, 1898
Died in Hollywood, California, 1937

American composer of popular songs, musicals, film scores, the opera Porgy and Bess, *and jazz orchestral works, including* Rhapsody in Blue *and* An American in Paris

ONE OF THE MOST FAMOUS EVENINGS in music history was February 12, 1924.

George Gershwin had accepted the invitation to write something for a special concert, and then he forgot about it. One day he was playing pool when his brother Ira came in with a newspaper article that told about an important concert one month away, on which George Gershwin was hard at work. Luckily, George Gershwin was one who worked well under pressure, and he produced *Rhapsody in Blue* on time.

The night of the concert was tense, the audience full of famous musicians, but Gershwin's music won thunderous ovations. Before he could acknowledge the applause, he had to bandage his hands. He had pounded the piano so hard there was blood on the keys.

While he was growing up, Gershwin assumed music was something girls did. He played stickball and baseball, and was the roller-skating champion of his neighborhood on the lower East Side of Manhattan. Then, at age ten, he heard a

classmate playing Antonin Dvorak's "Humoresque" for the younger grades. Suddenly he saw the beauty of music.

Though Gershwin's parents, Russian-Jewish immigrants, had bought a second-hand piano for his older brother, Ira, George was so eager that his parents let him take the lessons. He left school at sixteen and worked ten hours a day in music stores, demonstrating new songs and trying to get his own published. Gershwin's first hit—"Swanee"—was one of the earliest phonograph records ever made and sold over two million copies. At age nineteen, he had become rich and famous.

Ira became known as "Mr. Words," while George was "Mr. Music," and together they wrote successful Broadway musicals. The brothers lived in adjoining penthouses on Riverside Drive, with a wide view of the Hudson River. George's apartment had fourteen rooms, with a piano even in the gym. He owned every music book of the time, was a major art collector, and drove a Mercedes Benz.

"When I am in my normal mood," Gershwin said, "music drips from my fingers." More often than not, this was at night. Gershwin loved parties. He would play the piano at celebrity gatherings, come home, and write songs till dawn.

"Great, isn't it?" he'd say of his latest song. Gershwin was in love with his own music and talked about himself constantly. When being driven somewhere, he would say, "You've got *Gershwin* with you, so drive carefully."

Most people were charmed, not repelled. He dated glamorous actresses, though he never married; when a woman he liked married someone else, he would say, "I'd feel terrible if I weren't so busy."

He was proud of his tan and his muscular physique. He played golf, rode horses, went skiing, and played tennis with modern composer Arnold Schoenberg. When he started losing his hair, he bought a refrigerator-sized machine that was said to stimulate hair growth.

Gershwin could polish off a quart of ice cream in one sitting. But most of the time he had stomach problems and kept to a bland diet: toast, cereal, crackers, applesauce. He constantly smoked cigars.

In 1936, during a concert tour that ended in Los Angeles, Gershwin began having memory lapses and dizzy spells, with the sensation that he was smelling burning rubber. Six months later, he died of a brain tumor at age thirty-eight.

He had two funerals at the same time. At the start of services in Hollywood, all the movie studios shut down for a moment of silence in his honor. In New York, the funeral music was Bach, Beethoven, and *Rhapsody in Blue.*

♪ Some of Gershwin's best-known songs are "I Got Rhythm" (first sung by Ethel Merman), "Let's Call the Whole Thing Off" (Fred Astaire and Ginger Rogers), "Someone to Watch Over Me" (Gertrude Lawrence), and "They Can't Take That Away from Me" (Fred Astaire). Songs from the all-black opera *Porgy and Bess* include "Summertime," "I Got Plenty o' Nuthin'," "Bess, You Is My Woman Now," and "It Ain't Necessarily So."

♪ *Rhapsody in Blue* is one of the most frequently played orchestral works written by an American. It was influenced by Liszt, blues music, and the sounds of a train trip Gershwin took to Boston. He called it "a musical kaleidoscope of America — of our vast melting pot."

Traveling Troubadour

Woody Guthrie

born in Okemah, Oklahoma, 1912
died in Queens, New York, 1967

Songwriter, enormously important to modern American folk music—his thousand songs include "This Land Is Your Land" and "So Long, It's Been Good to Know You"

WOODY GUTHRIE WAS SMALL FOR HIS AGE and was made fun of at school. To keep classmates off his back, he entertained in the school yard each morning, playing the harmonica and dancing jigs.

Guthrie never did finish high school. Instead, after a series of tragedies had split up his family, he left Oklahoma at age sixteen for the open road.

For a time, Guthrie worked at a drugstore where the boss had a guitar. When there were no customers, he "pecked on it," trying to re-create the songs his mother had sung — country ballads, nonsense songs, lullabies.

Ideas for new songs came from street people, newspapers, books he read. A dusty little man with a guitar slung over his shoulder, Guthrie toured the country, singing on radio shows, at parties, and at political rallies. He was a rambling man in the traveling troubadour tradition.

He loved words and finding new ways to put them together (his father had played word games with him). He wrote songs on anything — napkins, paper bags, and wide sheets of paper in the extra-wide typewriter of his friend Lee Hays (from the folk-singing group the Weavers).

Guthrie had periods of nonstop creativity. He wrote twenty-six songs in one month — including "Roll On Columbia" and "Pastures of Plenty" — while working in Oregon on a documentary film. Once someone asked him where he was from, and within minutes he was writing "Oklahoma Hills," which became a country music standard.

In California, he sang for dust bowl refugees — with whom he especially identified. "So Long, It's Been Good to Know You" was about people who had left Oklahoma and other states, starting life over after dust storms caused them to lose their land, their jobs, and their homes. He wrote "Union Maid" — for ten years his most popular song — in support of the labor movement. "I Ain't Got No Home" was a reaction to a popular hymn called "This World Is Not My Home," which he felt led people to accept poor treatment. Another song that made him mad was Irving Berlin's "God Bless America," which struck him as unrealistic. His response was "This Land Is Your Land," now considered an honorary national anthem.

Woody Guthrie had a flat, dry voice, and was only an average guitar player. But

he had a way of performing that made people take notice. He was very funny, with a graceful Oklahoma drawl. One of his favorite ways of singing was the "talking blues," a black art form he excelled at.

He wore blue jeans and shaved when he felt like it. On the road, he also bathed when he felt like it. One time a friend picked him up and just plopped him in the bathtub. He smoked cigarettes constantly, and he was a walking suitcase, sometimes wearing five shirts at a time.

Guthrie married three times and had eight children. Restless and moody, he was on the road much of the time. He thought money corrupted people, and he often gave it away.

Guthrie was hospitalized most of the last fifteen years of his life, with a progressive nerve disease. He died at age fifty-five. The same year that he died, his twenty-year-old son recorded "Alice's Restaurant," the long talking blues that made Arlo Guthrie famous.

♪ Guthrie wrote many of his best songs ("The Car-Car Song," "Put Your Finger in the Air") for children. He compiled *Songs to Grow On* for his daughter Cathy. (Nicknamed Stackabones, she died at age four in a fire.) His children's albums have become standards in nursery schools everywhere.

♪ Guthrie considered "Tom Joad" (written for the film of John Steinbeck's *Grapes of Wrath*) the best song he'd written. On one of his radio shows he gave his musical philosophy: "I hate a song that makes you think that you are just born to lose . . . too old or too young or too fat or too thin or too this or too that. . . . I am out to sing songs that will prove to you that this is your world . . . no matter what."

♪ Robert Zimmerman started his career by learning hundreds of Guthrie songs. He held his guitar the way Guthrie did, invented a traveling past, and was pleased that his hair was curly like Guthrie's. He visited Guthrie in the hospital in 1961 and sang for him; by then he had changed his name to Bob Dylan.

Musical Terms

ballet — an art form that uses dancing, music, and scenery to tell a story

cantata — a long, usually religious work for chorus and orchestra

concerto — a work in three movements for solo instrument(s) and orchestra

folk song — a traditional song, composer unknown, passed from one generation to the next

invention — short keyboard composition using melodies independent of each other

libretto — the text of an opera

Mass — music to accompany the principal service of the Roman Catholic Church

mazurka — a Polish country dance

movement — a section of a larger musical work with a distinct beginning and end

opera — a drama in which most characters sing, with orchestral accompaniment

operetta — a comic opera

orchestra — a group of musicians, including string (such as violin and cello) players

overture — orchestral music introducing an opera or play

polonaise — a stately Polish dance

quartet — a piece of music written for four musicians

rag — a piece of ragtime music

ragtime — an early type of jazz, using "ragged" rhythm

repertoire — a list of pieces that a person or group is prepared to perform

requiem — a musical composition in honor of the dead

sonata — an instrumental work for one or two players in three or four movements of contrasting styles

symphony — a long work for orchestra usually in three or four movements

theme — the main melody of a musical work

variations — the repetition of a theme with changes in rhythm or style

waltz — a dance with a rhythm of one strong beat followed by two lesser beats

Index of Composers

*F*OR FURTHER READING . . . AND LISTENING

Baily, Leslie. *Gilbert and Sullivan: Their Lives and Times.* New York: Viking, 1974.

Barber, David. *Bach, Beethoven, and the Boys: Music History As It Ought to Be Taught.* Toronto: Sound and Vision, 1986.

Bookspan, Martin. *101 Masterpieces of Music and Their Composers.* Garden City, NY: Doubleday, 1973.

Borge, Victor. *My Favorite Comedies in Music.* New York: Watts, 1980.

Guthrie, Woody. "Three Hours of Songs and Conversation, Recorded by Alan Lomax in 1940." Cambridge, MA: Rounder Records, 1988.

Hammond, Susan, producer. "Beethoven Lives Upstairs," "Mr. Bach Comes to Call," and "Mozart's Magic Fantasy: A Journey through *The Magic Flute.*" Toronto: Classical Kids (recordings), 1988, 1990.

Haskins, James, with Kathleen Benson. *Scott Joplin.* Garden City, NY: Doubleday, 1978.

Howard, John Tasker. *Stephen Foster, America's Troubadour.* New York: Crowell, 1934.

Lebrecht, Norman. *The Book of Musical Anecdotes.* New York: Free Press, 1985.

Nichols, Janet. *American Music Makers: An Introduction to American Composers.* New York: Walker, 1990.

O'Shea, John. *Was Mozart Poisoned?: Medical Investigations into the Lives of the Great Composers.* New York: St. Martin's Press, 1990.

Plantamura, Carol. *Woman Composers.* Santa Barbara, CA: Bellerophon, 1986.

Schonberg, Harold. *The Lives of the Great Composers.* New York: W. W. Norton, 1981.

Schwimmer, Franciska. *Great Musicians as Children.* Garden City, NY: Doubleday, 1929.

Slonimsky, Nicolas. *The Concise Baker's Biographical Dictionary of Musicians.* New York: Schirmer, 1988.

Spaeth, Sigmund. *Stories Behind the World's Great Music.* Garden City, NY: Garden City Publishing, 1937.

Ventura, Piero. *Great Composers.* New York: Putnam, 1989.

Volta, Ornella. *Satie Seen through His Letters.* New York: Marion Boyers, 1989.

Zoff, Otto, ed. *Great Composers: Through the Eyes of Their Contemporaries.* New York: Dutton, 1951.

. . . *and recordings of music by composers in this book*